# The Trilogy

## I am NOT Responsible For Your Tears

## The Authentic Guide To Being Happy

*Maxi E. Norman*

# The Trilogy

## I am *NOT* Responsible for Your Tears

## The Authentic Guide to Being Happy

Maxi E. Norman

Copyright© 2023 By Maxi E. Norman

All rights reserved. No part of this book may be reproduced or used in any manner without **written** permission of the copyright owner except for the use of quotations in a book review.

For more information

Email address:
info@ElnoraMaxwell.com

FIRST EDITION

# Dedication

This book is dedicated to anyone who needs to HEAL from the apologies that you are owed but have yet to receive.

I am **SORRY**

Just know that

You Are **LOVED**

You Are **ENOUGH**

You Deserve to Be **HAPPY** 😊

# Living Life in Full Bloom 🌼

**Mommy We Made It!!!!!!!**

I do not think I can write or express enough how much I LOVE YOU. Your strong will and refusal to not give up is the reason I hustle hard every day. You are an example of what a strong woman looks like. Your love and dedication to your girls are why I can walk with my head held high. You are the reason why no one can break me. I pray that I am making you proud. I am glad you never gave up on me.

Thank you for believing in me even when you didn't understand my visions, or they did not make sense to anyone but me. Even when my truths made you mad, you encouraged me to keep writing. Through all of my hard-headedness.

I thank God, you still loved me enough to push through it with me. I will never be able to repay you for all you have done for me. Always know that I will forever Hold Us Down. It's only up from here.

Love Always,

Your Misunderstood Middle Child

Sometimes in life, we must be motivated to start, willing to heal, and be able to let it all go and simply CHOOSE ourselves if it means that we are not happy. On this journey called life, I have experienced so much that I come to realize that there is JOY in the journey.

I had to struggle and fight through this process to make it to what I now call my "*Happy Place*". I learned the hard way that nobody was coming to save me, nobody was going to fix the issues in my life but me.

I needed HELP!!!!!! Sometimes I needed a hug. Other times I needed to be pushed beyond my comfort zone to see that my life was not my own and to understand that I have gifts and experiences that I needed to share with the world.

My story, my life, and everything in between needed to be shared for me to heal. At first, writing my story felt like I was telling all my business to strangers, but I realized needed to be set free.

Once I started the healing process, I began to open up more. After I opened up, it seemed like the floodgates of my heart released and poured out of me. What happened next was so unexpected. I was triggered, like super triggered. I was in a place where I was feeling all the feels. I was pissed off at myself for starting this process. I was extra emotional crying all the damn time. I was over it. It was rough. I was fighting with myself because I felt like people in my life needed to be cut off. This hurt me deeply because I am not good at letting people go even if they hurt me. The result was that no matter what the triggers were, the hurt, the crying, or the sickness in my body, I was in pain. The facts were the facts.

Me choosing me and being happy was the only priority. I needed to be happy with myself. Happy with the journey, and happy with my past. Happy knowing that what I had endured in my life was not in vain, and happy knowing that I may have found my purpose.

Believing and knowing my purpose hopefully would help someone see that they too deserved to be happy.

Happiness is a choice. Happiness is something I'm choosing every day regardless of what troubles may come my way. We all deserve to be happy. We all deserve our Cinderella moment. You have slaved and suffered enough for everyone else and this time around IT IS all about YOU.

Welcome to The Trilogy.

7 is the number of completion. In my first book, I strived to encourage and motivate. In my second book, we cried. Lawd, did we cry, we grieved everything. However, we kicked started our process of healing. This is my third book, and it is only right that it is created to help you get to your HAPPY PLACE.

In this book, we will go through the 7 Steps to Becoming Happy.

Listen, no one is responsible for your tears. It is up to you. Yes, I said it. It is up to you to live a fulfilled life. You are in charge of your emotions. You get to live your life how you see fit.

Happiness is not something that will fall out of the sky and land in your lap, Happiness will not magically happen when your dream mate comes along and sweeps you off your feet. There is no other person that will make you happy if happiness isn't already dwelling inside of you.

So, move in a little closer and bring me your ear so you can catch this loud and clear. Not a single soul is responsible for making you happy. Being happy is a job that belongs to you. Being happy is always an option. It is a job that you must clock in to daily. It is an important life skill that you must master. You are not here to settle for mediocrity.

You deserve to be HAPPY.

Strap on your best boots and let's get it out of the mud!

Repeat this: *Through Hell or High Water I am going to live the rest of my life Happy.*

## Step 1: Stop Playing Victim

### (Who is to blame?)

Ok, life sucks. Let us start by getting the negativity out first. Mindset is everything. Life is happening, and it is not happening only to you. Finding true happiness starts from within. You will often hear people say that they are happy because the people they love are happy.

Raise your hand if you have heard this before or if you have said this often. In some cases, this can be true. But as a former people pleaser, when you are the giver, your happiness cannot be made by you solely giving and doing for others.

Riddle me this: Have you ever asked yourself why are you giving so much? Why do you give so much of yourself that you end up depleted?

Why would you give your last not knowing if people would do the same for you? Why would you sacrifice so much to place yourself in a bad situation? I used to hear folks say all the time that you shouldn't lend out stuff you can't afford to miss but we do it all the time with our time, our money, and our peace.

We just walk around giving and giving to no end. Now listen, not everyone falls into these categories. You perfect patties out here with it all figured out more power to you. But for those of us that don't have It figured out, we are not okay. It's time to really look at yourself in the mirror and take a mental recap of your life thus far.

Dig deep down into the pit of your soul and ask yourself why you do not have boundaries and what started you being this way.

I was so lost, I had it bad, just floating around lost in the sauce of giving. I was so lost that I did not even know if I was giving because it made me happy or if I had become so co-dependent on people needing me.

Was I just people-pleasing? Or was my need to feel needed that bad that I would just give, give, and give even when people were doing me bogus. When I started being honest with myself, I realized that I had been conditioned at an early age to be a giver or in many cases be the sacrificial lamb.

I was the one that went without, making sure others had it even when it hurt or even when I did not want to. That was my position. When you spend your whole life living to make everyone else happy you lose a part of yourself. I know I did. I felt resentful, angry, and disappointed.

I used to tell my sister all the time I wished I could be selfish, I felt like my life no longer belonged to me. I no longer felt like I even knew what I was supposed to be doing with my life. So, who is to blame?

It took me a long time to see that I was a people pleaser.

I always did what I was told. I wanted everyone around me to be happy. I watched the struggles my mom went through trying to raise 3 girls and working in a non-traditional field. In the 80s it was uncommon for women to be janitors, meter readers, fix washers and dryer machines, or to be a bus mechanic.

All these were jobs that my mom had and loved. I felt like the dirtier the job the better in my mom's eyes. What a lot of folks did not know was she got those jobs because she would fulfill the quota for affirmative action meaning she was a woman, and she was black, so she checked all the boxes.

Truth be told they did not want her to have those jobs. She was sexually harassed nonstop, and she would be paid lesser than her male counterparts. So, when it came to taking the stress off my mom, I turned into a perfectionist. I was told that at 3 years old I would not go anywhere without my clothes being ironed. I never wanted to be a disappointment.

I was 7 years old when it became my responsibility to make sure myself and my siblings were up and ready for school and to ensure that we made it home safely. We were latchkey kids. If you are not aware of what a latchkey kid is, it is kids left alone at home way before we were supposed to be.

I was also responsible for making sure our house stayed clean, particularly before my mom would get home from work. I remember being in elementary school and I would come home and do my homework but by the time my mom got home she found me in tears because I felt like my handwriting wasn't pretty.

I would spend hours rewriting it until it was perfect. I even accepted that I never got new clothes, shoes, coats, etc. I always made sure I took extra care of my stuff. That's just what I did. My mom never had to ask. It also did not help that I accepted having to be responsible seriously and to the extreme.

In my mind, I had to do it because who else was going to do it, right? Looking back, I was a full-on people pleaser. My childhood was great. My mom was outside playing in the dirt, doing cartwheels in the grass, going to the park type of mom. She wanted her girls to lack nothing,

She taught us how to change tires and fish with bamboo sticks. We had every toy imaginable. However, even with all the fun my responsibilities never changed. My grades never slipped. I had straight A's up until the 10th grade then it was all A's and B's.

My responsibilities trumped my feelings and how I was getting treated. I was teased and bullied about my name and my weight probably up until my junior year in high school.

I was so over everything that I was going through I convinced myself that the only way to find some relief was to go away to college. College was the way out. College would change everything about my current situation.

In my mind college would bring me happiness. I planned to focus on school.

Keep my head in the books, and make sure my sisters were cool. Then off to college, I go, far from this uncomfortable life. It was crazy that at 15 years old that you could already feel tired of life.

I did exactly what I said I would do. I kept my grades up all through high school even while holding down a job and going to vocational school for cosmetology. I was a naturally gifted hair braider. Braiding hair was a side hustle for me because I never really wanted to do hair.

Enrolling in hair school wasn't my sole choice, it was me doing what everyone else wanted me to do. DOING HAIR DID NOTHING FOR ME! It is why I dropped out of hair school with less than 500 hours left to get my license.

I graduated high at the top of my class. I also received multiple acceptance letters from different colleges, Clark Atlanta University and the University of Louisville were my final top two selections. I even had a few scholarship offers. Although my mom was excited and proud of me, when it came to what it would cost for me to go to college, was something different.

I was determined to make it happen. I graduated in May 1999. This was shortly after my oldest niece was less than a month old. (We weren't aware that my sister was pregnant nor were we prepared for her to bring a baby home).

When we finally made it to the hospital to meet my niece, we were all in shock because not only had my niece been a surprise but the same week my great-grandmother on my father's side had passed away, so it was an emotional week. Without being asked I instantly jumped into get-it-done mode.

My mom was in denial. She sat there looking at her first grandchild like she had seen a ghost. The next couple of days were all a blur. I had to prepare to attend a funeral and try and make sure my niece had everything she needed to come home.

Not knowing that my sister was pregnant we didn't have anything for the baby. I had to make it happen from baby beds to clothes to dressers.

My niece would never go without the things she needed and at this point 24 years later anything she wanted. After a couple of weeks, things seemed to calm down in my household.

My mom broke the news to me that going away to college was no longer an option for me. Not only could I not go away to college, but I needed to stay close to home and help take care of my niece.

This pissed me off. I was angry. I was bitter and the resentment was running deep down. I played my position; I did what everyone asked of me and all I wanted was to go away to school. I was heartbroken. I didn't understand why things just didn't pan out the way I wanted them to.

So, who's to blame? Me for not being selfish and putting myself first, was it my mom or my sister? Back then I didn't have a clue of what a boundary was, that was a foreign thing to me. Best believe the next couple of years I was angry. However, I was conditioned to accept less and people please.

The love for my family put me right back into go mode and so that's what I did. My niece was spoiled, I took care of her so much, I eventually became her guardian. She had to live with me off and on throughout her entire childhood. In the present day, she tells anyone who will listen that she is my one and only child. She and I had our years of struggling and we've had our years of tears.

She changed my life. She made me highly aware that someone was watching and expected me to be an example. She watched me daily, waiting for me to teach her what she needed to learn in this life.

Mae Mae, I hope you know I love you beyond the words in this book. You made me a better person. You have a way of always making me smile and brighten up my day.

You're one of my favorite people to be around. I'm so proud of the beautiful, fun-loving, smart, hard-working, woman you have turned out to be. These last 24 years have been a ball.

Watching you live your life to the fullest lets me know I at least got one thing right in my life. I will forever be here for you and Baby Steve.

Love you to the moon and back.

Your Favorite Auntie

I did not see my early 20s turning out the way they did. I was supposed to be in college far away from my family and their drama. However, looking back, I honestly don't know if I would have been able to function without being around my niece full-time and watching her grow up.

At one point in time, I felt like I was dealt a bad hand. I really could have played victim to my circumstances, but I wasn't raised like that. There weren't any woe-is-me moments. I couldn't sit and cry about it either. No one was responsible for my tears. My sister was fully capable of taking care of her child. My role in my family was always MAXI will do it. I allowed the people around me to be solely dependent upon me even if they didn't need me.

It has taken me 20 years to unlearn those bad habits.

Again, who's to blame? The answer is so clear to me now and the answer is no one!!! You can play the victim and think somebody or something will save you. When you are unaware of what a boundary is and why you need them in your life this tends to happen

You simply must give yourself grace. Parenting doesn't come with a handbook... My mom apologized years later; she told me that it was a mistake to not send me away to college. When you don't know, you don't know, life is about lessons. Your parents are just humans winging it. My mom was only trying to make it happen day to day. I recently started asking my friends and family what they think they would be doing in their 40s. A lot of them answered with "I never thought that far ahead". Now that we are all in our 40s, we know our lives are supposed to be better than it is.

I always wanted to go away to college, but I never had a clear career path. When I started college locally, I enrolled in school for accounting. I feel like I only wanted to do accounting because one of my aunts chose that career path and she was very successful.

I had a love for numbers but having a job in finance, sitting at a desk inside a cubicle made me realize I couldn't imagine doing that for 20 years, especially in Corporate America.

Now I know that to be HAPPY, I need to revisit some of my different DREAMS because this is not going to cut it. I realized working 10 to 50 years for a company making someone else's family rich and building their family legacy was not going to do anything for my family.

Back to my point of playing victim to your own BS, it ultimately leaves you sobbing in your tears. It doesn't matter if you are 23 or 53 you can always choose HAPPY.

Choose to start over, dream a different dream, and set new goals. Start with a short-term goal, gradually add on to it and T turn it into a long-term goal. God intended for you to live a happy life.

Step 1: Identify what makes you unhappy. You have the right to be mad, scream, and even cry about it. Do what you need to do to get it out of your system. Next, take the steps to change it. It starts with your mindset. Simply viewing a situation in a positive light can change everything.

If you only see something as a negative thing, that's what it will be, the choice is yours. As the old saying goes you either shit or get off the pot. I've taken this to mean that you either let it go and choose happy or shut up and stop complaining about being unhappy. The only person you will have to blame is you.

## Step 2: Choose Life
### (There is Always Something to Live For)

Your life is valuable no matter how rough it gets.

Lately, whether it is via T.V., radio, podcast, or social media it is always something constantly trending regarding mental health. Mental health has become the forefront of a lot of conversations. Growing up mental health was frowned upon, the answer to mental health was "You're Crazy". Nobody bothered to dig into what you were going through or even bothered to ask, they just labeled you crazy. Many people nowadays are taking mental health more seriously which is amazing.

A lot of my childhood trauma came from not being protected. I felt that as a parent your #1 job and priority is to protect your kids from harm. However, when it came to me that was not the case.

I would get triggered easily and when something got under my skin, I would lose my mind. When it came to my dad's side of the family my mom would allow outside people to talk about me or judge my character. She would not defend me when they would tell a lie about me or talk bad about me. I was told that the reason she never defended me was because they did that to everyone else so it shouldn't have been a big deal, but it was to me.

When I was younger, I was labeled, as angry, stuck up, nonchalant, or simply mean.

I began to label myself as the misunderstood mean girl. Once I did the work on myself and understood what mental health was, I was finally able to put a word with my emotions. I was depressed, had anxiety and I was even suicidal. The first time I ever thought about committing suicide I was in the 5th grade. *There is a chapter dedicated to this traumatic experience.* That experience made me feel worthless. It made me believe my life didn't mean much to anyone, especially me.

I had another brush with suicide when I was laid off from a job that I was employed with for 5 years. I had no clue what I was going to do next. I worked so many jobs in my life before I got that job. I was finally happy I found a job that I was not only good at but that I loved.

It was also my first real job In Corporate America. I recall sitting on my couch with one of my childhood friends telling her that I could just kill myself. I told her the only thing stopping me from doing it was that I knew it would hurt quite a few people.

My family life was in shambles, and if I could have ensured that my oldest niece would be set for life, I probably would have done it. There was so much drama within my family that the only JOY I experienced in life was seeing my niece happy every day. Suicidal thoughts came and went throughout my life. The one time I did attempt suicide, God and my youngest sister saved my life.

I visited my mom's house, and we had it out. I was already going through my mental breakdown earlier that day. The argument with my mom got so bad that it could have turned physical. My youngest sister would always try to talk me off the ledge and she always tries to get me to say fuck them people regardless of who they are. I can be extra sensitive sometimes and back then I had to get my point across even if it was through cursing and screaming.

After all the fussing was over, I was pissed. I went to the bathroom and took a bunch of pills. I was so angry between my screams and cries. I don't remember but I must have told my sister what I had just done and that I was planning on going home to take some more pills. I was praying not to wake up.

I scared her so badly that she refused to let me leave. She was my shadow; she had taken to heart what my mom told her. *You have sisters, you don't need friends.*

Besides crying and making me vomit, my sister trapped me in her room and held me. She prayed and cried over me the whole night. The next day she came to my house to empty every pill and medicine that I had.

My sister chose life for me that day, I was out of my mind. She saved me and she made me realize that I was loved.

Step 2: Life Is Hard.

Loving Yourself and valuing life sometimes can be overwhelming. You must Love yourself. Hell, you must over-love yourself. You must love yourself enough to get help. You must put 10x as much effort into working on your inside, the same effort you put into making the outside part of you look good.

You cannot fake happiness through this thing called LIFE. It makes absolutely no sense to be cute on the outside and rotten as hell on the inside.

Everyone's journey is different whether your route is therapy, medication, or prayer. Loving yourself wholeheartedly is the goal. When I found my Happy Place, I learned to love and accept every flaw; including the pieces of grey hair growing around my edges down to my second toe which happens to be longer than my big toe. I know that sounds crazy, but I used to be subconscious about it, and I used to get teased about it.

People will find anything to make you feel bad when they are not happy within themselves. This road to happiness is not an easy process with no straight path. You must put in a lot of work. Throughout this process getting the help I needed allowed me to become aware of my triggers. I can talk myself out of feeling depressed now.

Keeping my faith strong allows me to always believe there is a better day coming tomorrow. No one will LOVE YOU MORE than you. Self-work requires you to do self-care.

Every day you are blessed to open your eyes is another day you must choose HAPPINESS and make today better than yesterday.

## Step 3: Let It Go
## (Don't Stay Stuck)

The best advice I received in my adult life was "Don't allow your past trauma to hold your present life hostage".

I was bullied about everything from my name to my height to my weight, to being smart, to loving to read books. Being bullied constantly never bothered me much. But when it came to repeatedly getting teased about my name, I would lose it.

As early as 5 years old I was called Maxi Pad, or Kotex, or tampons even period girl. Lawd that burned me to my core. I wanted to change my name to anything but Maxi, it sucked.

Being confident was something I had to learn early in life. Besides being teased about my name I had to deal with my physical body changing as well. My hips grew way before they should have.

I never could dress like the girls my age because I could never fit the bottoms.

Plus-size clothes didn't come in as many options as they do today. I was also a tomboy growing up, so dickies and Pelle Pelle T-shirts were my jam.

My dad would always tell me that I was the smartest, prettiest girl in the world and that I had better believe it was because I looked just like him and no one could tell me anything different. I knew I was smart and cute.

By the 5th grade, fashion and music had taken over my life. I fell in love with all genres (music country, hip hop, jazz, and R&B) just to name a few. I also fell in love with denim, and I am still in love with it today.

I remember wanting to have my bang cut like left eye from TLC. I cut my hair without permission (too short) and I messed it up so badly.

My mom cursed me out and fixed it all at the same time, but that didn't stop me. When my bang grew back, I figured out what I did wrong the first time and I eventually got my left eye bang.

My obsession with denim got so bad that I started cutting up old clothes and making my Barbie dolls outfits. One day during a search for clothes to cut up, I came across a two-piece denim outfit that my mom owned. It was light denim with white stitched flower patterns all over the pants and the jacket.

I was like a size 7/8 and all I could think of is how I needed to fit into this outfit by the next school year. I asked, no I begged my mom to let me have the outfit. She said no because I wanted to cut it up to make more doll clothes. I explained to her that I wanted to wear it and she still said no, mainly because I couldn't fit it.

I was finally able to convince my mom to bet me that if I could get into the outfit, she would let me have it. Me being me, I love a good friendly competition. I must win and you best believe I won the bet and got the outfit.

I was super excited about winning that outfit, but that excitement was short-lived. I shared a room with my younger sister my whole life and I normally never would sleep in the living room. Plus, my younger sister never allowed me to do anything alone.

But she cared nothing about my obsession with fashion or music. She wanted nothing to do with staying up with me and recording music videos on VHS tapes. Back then music videos only came on late at night. In between recording songs off the radio onto cassette tapes in the living room. I fell asleep on the couch and was awakened by a grown man on top of me pinning me down and covering my mouth making it hard to breathe trying to rape me. I went into shock and froze for what seemed like forever then I snapped out of it and began fighting for my life. I was trying hard to swing and punch and kick until I was able to break free.

I couldn't believe it I ran down the hallway in my ripped pajamas to my bedroom and locked the door. A couple of days later this same person tried to trap me in a corner in the kitchen and told me that they were drunk the other night.

I grabbed a knife just in case he was going to try something again. I was not going to freeze up this time and he was going to lose his life if he tried something again.

From that day forward I was never caught slipping again. I was never anywhere in that house alone and never let my siblings be either. Sleeping was no longer an option, and I would only sleep for 2 or 3 hours at a time.

Even now I'm always up at all times of the day and night. I barely sleep and I associate this with what happened to me. I believe that if I never wanted that denim outfit and decided to lose weight this would have never happened to me.

I was 11 years old when I got violated and I didn't know what to do or how to feel. So, I did nothing and told no one. I just protected myself and my siblings. I didn't sleep and I carried weapons within the house from knives to padlocks. I was never caught in a room in that house alone and most definitely gained the weight back that way no one else would look at me like that.

As I got older, I would hear people saying stuff like she is super pretty and would be fine as hell if she lost some weight. I took that as a compliment. It took me until I was in my late 20s to ever speak on this even then I only told my younger sister and she had to swear to the high heavens to never say anything to anybody.

For many years I blamed myself. It got so bad that I wanted to die. I remember I could open my bedroom window and crawl out to the roof of the house. I would climb out the window and sit on the roof many nights. Sometimes I would lay on the roof with my eyes closed and imagine falling off to end it all.

But for whatever reason anytime I would be laying there with my eyes closed my younger sister would come busting into our room yelling at me. She would come to the window yelling Maxi get your crazy ass off that damn roof!

I thank God for her daily. Without her plus God sparing my life and restoring my peace as well as my purpose, I probably would not be here.

Honestly, this whole book came to life because I was told my abuser died. For whatever reason hearing his name triggered me. I couldn't understand why I felt nothing. I told myself that if I am getting triggered, I am not fully healed from that situation.

That pissed me off because in my mind I did the work. When I first started writing this book, I completely wanted to delete this whole chapter and figure out what else to write about.

But clearly, this story had to be told, I needed to release the trauma from my life. I no longer wanted to be held hostage to something that wasn't my fault. I wanted freedom from that. I wanted to be set free.

Step 3: Your past is exactly what it is in your past. No more allowing people to throw it in your face. No more being ashamed. No more covering it up and sugar-coating stuff to spare someone else's feelings.

Let it Go and Go Live a Happy Life.

To my Sissy Pooh:

Our daily talks and your consistent harassment my entire life have been the push I needed to LIVE. I love you more than those baby goats you send me every day on Tik Tok. Although there have been times you may have felt I didn't want you following me around and copying everything I do. Just know that you're the best shadow a girl could ask for. If I had the option to pick someone else as a sister, I would pick you a million times again and again. You are my real-life guardian angel.

*Your Bestie & Twin*

## Step 4: Restart, Reset, Release
## (Lawd, I'm Locked Up)

In life, we can be afraid to start over because if you are not careful, you will be forced to sit down and when that happens the recovery is harder.

I am a giver. I've been giving and giving my whole life. I believe that giving is my superpower. When you continue to give and give some more. You will give so much of yourself that you have nothing left for yourself.

As for me, I am hardheaded. I will continue to push myself beyond my limits. My sit-down moments used to mean falling ill all the time. I would end up in the hospital. I would only get a couple of days rest and some meds, Then back to business as normal.

For the last 4 years, I've had a ringing in my left ear. It has caused me to lose my hearing. Somedays it's so loud that it causes me to have migraines. I'm aware that sometimes you just must push through the pain.

I currently have carpal tunnel in my right hand. At times my right hand hurts so bad that the pain shoots up my arm into my shoulder but I'm still here pushing through. I have seen multiple specialists, but nothing stops this hustle.

When I get sit-down moments, Baby the world stops. LOL

In life, you need to try a bunch of different things to see what you like and to see what you're good at. However, this mindset has contributed to my quitting and getting fired from multiple jobs.

But no one of them has stopped the hustle. I attended college to study in multiple fields until I finally realized that I like being behind the scenes.

This realization landed me back in Corporate America working for a huge pharmaceutical company as an executive assistant to a VP. Even though it limited my number of tattoos, this was a sweet job and I loved it. I was sad for it to end; I was laid off after 1-year.

After I was laid off, I vowed to just chill out for a few months and try not to stress about what to do next. My first couple of weeks were easy and breezy. I applied for unemployment and signed up for some classes.

Before I could continue, I was forced into another sit-down moment. Transparent Moment: I almost didn't tell this story because a lot of my family wanted to pretend like it never happened. The truth of the matter is it happened to me not them.

It's a part of my release. That is why I was able to Rest and Restart. Remember this: Never let someone else's fear, shame, and or disappointments stall your healing. Never allow anyone to silence you or steal your voice for any reason.

I was off work maxin and relaxing and it was starting to warm up outside plus concerts were poppin' off everywhere. I and a few of my friends decided we were going to drive to Wisconsin to go see Future and Rico Love in concert. We had a ball! A couple of days later I was cleaning my car and noticed that the guy my friend was currently seeing had left his bottle of cologne in my car. I reached out to my friend and let her know I had it. She stated that she was already in my area and that she would swing by to pick it up.

I was aware that lately my friend was being stalked. The tires on her vehicle were flattened while she was at work and my car had been egged. She was taking precautions to protect herself. She stops by my house to pick up the cologne so she can drop it off.

I was cleaning up and still had on pajama clothes. She asked me to ride with her, so I could also pick up some food plus the drop-off was close to my house. Pretty much as soon as we pulled up to her guy's house a car speeds up out of nowhere to block us.

A guy jumps out of the car with a bat and starts swinging the bat at her vehicle. He started yelling at us to get out of the vehicle. The girl driving is holding a couple of weapons and started yelling for us to get out of the vehicle as well.

My friend and I are sitting in the vehicle in disbelief laughing like what the fuck is happening. My friend calls her guy to come outside. The girl in the car starts yelling that she has finally caught my friend after all her stalking.

This pissed me off and I yelled out the window are you fucking stupid, and this is some stupid shit. The guy with her became more enraged, he began to hit the car we are in aggressively with the bat.

After about 5 minutes My friend and I collectively decided that we had enough of this BS. So, we presented a weapon of our own and ordered them to move their car.

Now put the book down for a second and then come back with a clear open mind. Don't be acting like a lawyer or a judge (we were both concealed to carry) and I know the biggest question is why didn't we just call the police, right?

Well over the years I had my fair share of run-ins with the police and it didn't turn out great. I watched them snatch the young guys in my neighborhood off the street and beat them. I was pulled over multiple times and I was harassed because of the car I was driving, (they felt I was too young and too black to be driving it).

Plus, I believed that the stalker girl and dude with the bat pulled up on us to fight or to scare us and either way, it wasn't about to go down the way they thought.

The stalker and her sidekick believed they had the upper hand until we rolled the window down and point a gun at them, we nicely asked her to move the fucking car and for him to stop swinging the bat or else.

The sidekick with the bat dropped it quickly then took off running up the street screaming Oh My God Oh My God they got a gun. The stalker quickly pulled off to catch the screaming guy and yelled she was calling the police.

I was at a loss for words. How are you calling the police on us when you are the one stalking and rolling up wielding weapons? How? This was just unbelievable.

We sat there for a minute in my friend's vehicle trying to decide whether we were going to just sit and wait for the police or leave.

We drove a couple of blocks, but we were pulled over and surrounded by multiple police cars.

The cops jump out with their guns drawn, yelling at us asking where the guns are. My car door was snatched open, with guns still drawn and pointed at me. The cop rudely asked me again where the guns were. I responded *I don't know what you are talking about sir*. I was commanded to get out of the vehicle. I was immediately handcuffed, pushed into the cop car, and the officer sped off. I was taken to the local police station and placed in a holding cell by myself. I was left there for a few hours. I had no idea what happened to my friend or where she was, and she hadn't been placed in a holding cell either.

I'm guessing it was a few more hours before I heard my friend's voice. I yelled out to her to see if she was okay. She replied and said that she was okay and that she had been sitting in a room with a detective explaining to him everything. All I could say was damn I have been sitting in this cell the whole time.

A few moments later a cop comes to get me and takes me into a room. A detective walks in, sits down across from me, and says now tell me what happened?

I rolled my eyes; I wanted my phone call. He repeated his statement and asked again what happened.

I replied and said can you read me my rights? And what are my charges? I guess my line of questioning was making him mad because the detective turned to read me my rights. He said you are being charged with aggravated assault and illegal possession of multiple firearms.

I started laughing and said hell no you got me fucked up, for all of this mess should have stomped the stalker out but since I didn't touch the bitch, I don't have shit to say to you. He got even more mad and left the room. Another officer came to get me to take me straight back to my cell.

My friend asked what I said, I told her what happened, and she laughed she said your ass is crazy. Remember when I mentioned the many previous jobs I worked? One of them was finally paying off.

I once worked at the courthouse with paralegals doing research for cases. I also worked for the Association of

Lawyers in our area and met pretty much all of them.

During this time, I was forced to learn about our local laws. I learned a lot.

which meant talking to the police was not an option.

After what seemed like forever a set of new officers came in to check in on us. I was finally taken to get my mug shot and was able to get my phone call.

Back in the good old days of pay phones and pagers, I was good at remembering everyone's phone number. However now that I'm locked up, I was struggling to recall one number. Finally, I remembered one, it was a friend. I called her to tell her I was in jail and to please call my sister for me.

I wanted to let my sister know so she could inform my mom. Also, inform them not to worry because the officer that took my mug shot informed me that I would probably be able to get out on a signature bond since I had never been in trouble before.

Although she thought that I was lying, I had to repeatedly tell her that this was my life now. After my call, I was taken back to my cell and given a tv dinner.

Once back in my cell, I started pacing the floor and I repeatedly kept asking what time it was. I was told that I needed to relax. Who relaxes in jail? I wasn't crying but I was scared, I was mad as hell.

Thinking about the charges, I knew they had been trumped up. The next morning, I was handcuffed, placed in a police car, and taken downtown to the big courthouse.

I was charged with 4 felonies during my court hearing and my bond was $50K. The stalker girl lied to the police, told them we had multiple guns, and chased her down the street. None of this ever happened! She never showed up to court or pressed charges.

She just kicked off a lot of drama and tried to ruin our lives for no reason.

Although she didn't show up to court or press charges, the state picked up the cases anyway because it was a case that they could win. After court, I was placed in a holding cell again alone.

My friend and I spoke briefly regarding her grandmother stepping up to pay my bond to get out, but I told her no. I did not want to be in debt for bond money and figure out how to get a lawyer too.

After a while, it seemed like they forgot about me in that cell. I could hear multiple people being taken to use the phone and given food. Not me though, I was just left there alone for hours. I was finally escorted to get another mug shot and I was also able to make a phone call. It was nighttime by then and that pissed me off because I had court at 9 am and it was already past 7 pm.

I tried calling my sister and mom, once I got on the phone with them, they were freaking out so bad that they got on my nerves, so I hung up on them.

I was thankful that I was allowed to sit in a lobby area rather than go back to the holding cell. It was clear to me now that I was going to be booked and taken to another cell. I sat there just staring at the floor.

Once I was booked, I was taken through a door to a room and told to strip fully naked. I was told to bend over and cough. All the degrading things that one might see on tv happened to me. I was given a new outfit and taken to my cell.

I was placed in a cell all alone again. It didn't hit me that I was in jail until the next morning. To add fuel to the fire a custodian came in to wake me up so he could mop the floor with dirty mop water. To top it off, I received a visit from a social worker.

*I was starting to get a headache because I refused to drink the water. The sink is connected to the toilet and something about that just didn't sit right with me.* Plus, I decided not to eat the food either.

In my mind everyone had me messed up and this social worker is in my cell asking me a series of questions (mostly about my mental health) and also if I had people on the outside that loved me. Somewhere in the middle of her questions, I blurted out Damn I'm locked up like for real like I'm in really in jail.

The social worker looked at me strangely and finished her line of questioning then left me sitting on that metal bed with the itchy cover.

The next couple of days felt like a nightmare and I remained mad at my family because they weren't listening to me, and I continued to hang up on them. The reason I was hanging up on them was because they were still freaking out and making things about them.

They were too much in their feelings and doing what they wanted to do. They were acting like it was them that was locked up, not me.

After about a week of not eating and not talking to my family. I realized that I was sat down for a reason and why nothing was going the way that it should go.

I spent my whole life running around like a chicken with their head cut off. Going and going, over and beyond for others and all I needed in this moment was for people to listen to me.

I also realized that I was not listening to them either and it was my anger that had me sitting in jail for a little over a month. I clearly didn't understand how people continue to repeat criminal activity to keep going back to jail. This is it for me, my one-and-done!

I finally got a lawyer and made bail. Once I got out of jail my family went back to life as if nothing happened. I was different now. I was back all alone. No one even asked how things were going with the case and I had to figure out how to pay for my lawyer without a job.

Because of my pending felony charges, no one would hire me. With all the jobs I worked during that time in my life, I think I had the most background checks run on me. The funny thing was that I would go on interviews, get the job and the people would be so nice to me. But as soon as my background check would come back, they would do a whole 360, talk to and treat me ridiculously horrible.

God gave me Grace. I beat my case and outside of having an arrest record my background was now clear. The whole time while fighting my case I was unemployed and depressed. However, I never lost anything, not my car, not my place to stay, not my phone, nothing got cut off. I stood on the fact that God's favorites have it the hardest and I'm hardheaded. I needed to be sat down and isolated to receive what I needed.

Step 4: Restart Reset Release

To fully stand in your happiness and live you will have to face some things head on and you may even have to do them alone. When I got home from jail, I took a 2-hour shower. I felt dirty and, at that moment, I scrubbed and scrubbed until the water was cold, I cried.

I had to release whatever anger and hurt I had built up over all these years. I knew a reset was coming and I was about to partake in a new journey alone. There were moments when I struggled through this because everyone around me was back to their normal scheduled program.

I had to believe in myself. Believe in my inner strength. There were times I wouldn't talk or leave my bed. I was over life and its hardships. My sit down was for me to restart. I was giving away more of myself to other people than I was giving to myself. I needed to STOP.

I needed me more than anyone else did and although people close to me wouldn't understand, it needed to be done. I deserved to be HAPPY.

I now know that no matter if it was good or bad everything is working together for my greater good.

## Step: 5 Acceptance
### (All My Babies)

Choosing HAPPY every day is tough. To think that you will wake up happy every day and everything will be sunshine and rainbows with glitter on them is absurd. We never know what the day will bring our way. Let alone what will happen that may negatively affect our moods. That's why choosing happiness is a conscious decision that we must make every day. You must find that positivity in every situation.

I had the pleasure of being a bonus parent and a Godparent for the last 24 years. I have 3 nieces, 1 nephew, 5 God kids as well as a God niece and nephew. Also, a handful of other kids call me Auntie because I am a part of their lives in some form or fashion.

I always loved kids. I used to say I wanted six kids. I loved the thought of having a big family. I used to babysit my little cousins, I even worked as a camp counselor one summer too.

I would often say when I retired, I would go into the school system and become a kindergarten teacher. At one point I was taking classes to be a director of a daycare facility. This is how much I loved kids and wanted to be around them. Sometimes we must accept that something just isn't in the cards.

Growing up I always had difficult periods. As a teenager, I always had bad cramps. It would get so bad that sometimes I was unable to move and to top it all off my periods were extra heavy.

I would be curled up on the floor rocking back and forth popping Tylenol and holding a heating pad to my stomach. I used to feel like I was being punished because my two sisters never had any of the issues I had. As I got older, I would talk to my female family members, I learned that a lot of them had similar or more severe issues and they all had to have surgeries.

Some even had full hysterectomies by the age of 40 years old. By the time I was 20 years old, I had to see a specialist. I was told that they found a cyst in my uterus that had to be removed and tested to make sure it wasn't cancer. Next, my OBGYN found out I was anemic and placed me on iron pills plus birth control to try and fix the heavy bleeding.

T iron pills messed up my stomach and the birth control made my periods worse. I bled for 9 weeks straight. I was losing so much blood that I passed out while I was driving.

I was bleeding through pads left and right. I was bleeding so much I was bleeding through my clothes. It was the most embarrassing and scary thing at the same time. I consulted with my doctor, and his only suggestion was for me to take another set of birth control along with the set of birth control I was already taking. That didn't make sense to me, so I got a second opinion and changed doctors immediately.

My new doctor was very detailed. She ran every test there was to run to figure out what was going on with me. Age confirmed that I was severely anemic. I had uterine fibroids, endometriosis, and a cyst on my cervix that had to be removed.

Over the next ten years, I tried everything including multiple surgeries and biopsy. I tried different birth control (the pills, the shot, and the IUD. Nothing stopped my heavy periods which caused my anemia to worsen. It caused me to have blood transfusions, and iron shots became part of my normal routine.

By the time I was 35, it had gotten so bad my only option was either to continue to deal with it or have surgery. The surgery would mean that the chances of me being a mommy would never happen.

I would be a liar if I said I wasn't heartbroken. I always wanted to be someone's mommy. Some things just aren't in the cards. I had to choose me in that instance to have a happy life. I had to accept that birthing a child may never happen. It took me a while to realize that I would have to settle for just being someone's fine stepmom, auntie, and Godmother.

Life doesn't always go as planned. What's the saying? *Want to make God laugh, tell him your plans.* Accepting something does not mean that it still doesn't hurt at times. It's ok to be sad sometimes. You just can't stay sad. I still really love kids. I'm still one of those people who sees a newborn and wants to hold them and hold them close to your chest.

I'm just playing the cards of life that were dealt to me. I'm still choosing Happy. Hopefully, through my writings, author talks, and school speaking events, I can reach and help one person. I will be able to tell myself job well done.

I pray all my babies know how much they mean to me. I wouldn't be the person I am today without them. You'll keep me on my toes. I'm so proud of you'll and the people you'll are turning out to be. I'm truly blessed to have been a part of you'll lives. I Love Ya'll for Life.

## Step 6: Put Yourself First

### (Loyal By Default)

Value your time. Value your time. Loyalty, Loyalty, Loyalty. I can hear Kendrick Lamar and Rihanna's songs playing over and over again in my head as I am writing this chapter. Ride or Die Chick and Loyalty by default are now two phases that I have come to hate. I was loyal by default. Ride or Die Chick. I was holding people down regardless of how I felt they did me. If they were rocking, I would be rolling period.

Now if you happened to find your tribe and they care about you then being a Ride or Die type of person is not a problem. But life sometimes shows us that not everyone needs to go with you on this journey of life. People aren't even able to love you back the way you deserve to be loved.

Many times, people are unaware of how to love properly. A lot of times they don't love themselves enough. People often throw around the question, were you raised on love or survival?

As for me, I was raised with a little bit of love and a whole lot of survival. I know my parents loved me. They just had a funny way of showing it. You realize once you're an adult that your parents are just human folks trying to figure it out.

They were in survival mode all the time. Survival mode makes you a hustler, and a go-getter. It makes your priorities way different. Survival mode makes you wake up in a world where all your needs are not met.

You worry if you are going to get put out and must move again. You worry if the utilities were going to be cut off. You know what it feels like to hand wash your clothes out in the bathtub. And either hang them to dry or if you are lucky enough to live in an older house or apartment that had a big radiator heater you could lay them on to dry faster. You never had to heat your house with the oven door open.

Have you ever had to boil water to fill up a bathtub to take a bath? Survival mode makes you have tough skin. It makes your heart a little hard. It could even turn up your I don't give a fuck attitude extra early in life.

Being raised on survival may have caused you all types of traumas in your childhood.

A lot of things we have gone through have made us strong. But a lot of things don't prepare you for relationships.

Trauma can cause you to trauma bond with people with relatable experiences. You will look past the red flags. Your attraction will be strong because you have so much trauma in common. Don't get me wrong, it is possible to meet someone and connect with them and it be can beautiful.

But we are not here to chat about those relationships. Those are not relationships where you question yourself and can ultimately lose yourself to a point that you don't even recognize who you are.

We are here to talk about the trauma bonds that have you stuck. You know those relationships that you hear people say we've been together 15 years, etc. But in all that time there has been no progress. Maybe you want to be married, have kids, buy a house, or even start a new business.

Ya'll still be in the same place having the same argument and falling out about the same stuff all the time. Now I'm no relationship expert but I do know doing the same thing and excepting something to change is insane.

I have been insane for a time or two. And let's be clear this doesn't just apply to romantic relationships either. Some of us have been in a chokehold for years by friends and family as well.

Some of us have held on to friendships past the expiration date just because we have been friends since we were kids. And since you'll were kids, they've been selfish and inconsiderate. The relationship has always been one-sided.

A lot of these relationships outgrow each other and neither person is willing to walk away. Whether it is because of fear, loneliness, or something deeper. No one deserves to be unhappy or to have people in their lives that mean them no good. Why not choose happiness and let it go?

Or maybe you're like me when I was insane and just decided to settle because I felt like the dating pool was full of piss. Or maybe for a moment in time, you thought this was as good as it was going to get. Hell, at least some of your needs were being met right?

At one point in time, I thought to be like other people I knew were they just cheated and found their happiness in another person, but I wasn't like that and couldn't muster up the courage to do so I just sat in my misery because sometimes it not what other say to us it's the things, we tell ourselves that have us stuck or being mistreated.

We really must ask ourselves, is this Love or Lust? Why are we allowing someone to treat us in a way that we don't deserve? I know sometimes we come into relationships with baggage.

I know the unhealed me came into my past relationships with a 3-piece luggage set and a tote bag. Packed full to the point that the zipper might break. Those bags were full of trauma, heartache, and trust issues. All of which will have you stuck/ unable to let go of anything.

I'm the first to admit that letting people go and cutting folks out of my life was hard for me. When I love you, I love you, that's it for me. Even if you do me wrong, I would still ride for you. Being loyal by default is a mentality that will have you mistreating yourself.

It will have people telling you stuff like I didn't ask you to do that. After you have already gone above and beyond for them.

When you decide that enough is enough and you choose you and start to do things, saying no to things that no longer serve you and you start to heal you become more self-aware of the people you choose to have in your life.

Your Friends are a choice.

Your Mates are a choice.

Your family may not be a choice because you don't get to pick them, but you do get to choose to deal with them if they are not treating you right.

You don't have to subject yourself to misery and sit around being triggered by family members who don't want to change or heal from their traumas.

You choose the people you spend your time with.

You choose the people you exchange energies with. These are all choices.

When you choose yourself and choose happiness don't be surprised if your circle changes as you grow it is supposed to.

Step 6: You must reevaluate where, when, and what you are spending your time on. Time is one of the most expensive things you cannot afford to just give away. Once you give away your time you must know you're not getting it back.

Relationships are not meant to be hard. They are sometimes but you must work at them every day and the relationship with yourself is a must. Watch how your inner thoughts and feelings about you affect your choices.

You only get out what you put in. Don't get trauma bonded to someone or even something that is not serving your soul. Happiness is something you deserve in your lifetime.

Being happy is something you need in your life. I realized that the good and even the bad relationships had all taught me a lesson. I learned a lot about myself.

Have you ever sat and thought about the relationship you have been in and just got mad at yourself? Like what in the hell was going on with me internally that I allowed myself to accept what I did? What would allow me to be with someone that doesn't treat me right? What is allowing me to let my family do me any type of way and then expect me to still do for them?

How could you allow someone to mistreat you and think that because they love bombed you with time affection, money, or gifts that's ok? They played into your insecurities and trauma and vulnerabilities to build you up only to break you and tear you down.

The trauma and the drama will physically, emotionally, and mentally crush you. It makes that self-love and healing journey extremely important.

Stop faking happiness and being strong and showing up for everyone else and everything but yourself. Having people think that you're happy and living the life when you are home crying yourself to sleep at night.

Listen, no one is responsible for your tears. Don't be too prideful that you don't get the help you need. Healing looks different for everyone. You don't have to be great to start you just have to start to be great. Showing up in this world as a whole happy human is what matters the most.

This coming from someone who had to heal their own heart to become happy. Through the trauma, the drama, heartache, and pain. Through the tears and all the apologies, I deserved and have never received. I had to find the closure that I needed because the other people couldn't give that to me. I pray that sharing my experiences and journeys throughout my life sheds some light to help someone see the pot of gold at the end of their rainbow.

It's so much always going on in this world that you just need to simply ask yourself, why wouldn't you want to be happy?

## Step 7: Choose Happy

### (Beauty For My Ashes)

Seven is the number of completions. I know and I am living proof everything happens for a reason. Everything is working out for my good. When coming up with the title for this it came about because I had been crying about ending a relationship with someone I loved, and they told me to please stop crying because they didn't want to be responsible for my tears. That hit me like a ton of bricks. It let me know even when people hurt you or it hurt for you to choose yourself, they are not responsible for your emotions in any way.

You must feel all your feelings and you cannot control the actions of other people. All my test is now my testimony. I no longer hide my flaws I live out loud. I tell my stories to all people too and understand that you are not alone. We all have things we are not proud of, even ashamed of some things.

You may even be afraid to share things about your life. All of that is ok. My life, my story is perfectly imperfect. I can still live my life happily without any regrets. I was told that because I was so angry, so unhappy that I should either find someone to talk to about it or write about it and let it go.

I tried talking about it in therapy and I felt like I ended up being more misunderstood and more judged. So, to heal how I needed to heal writing became my art plus outlet. Writing allowed me to be free. Free from my pain. Free from my past. Free from anything that felt like it would keep me stuck. I no longer wanted to be unable to move forward with my life and live. Not just exist.

I have cried all the tears I needed to cry to be set free. God gave me the Beauty for my Ashes. The ashes on the crown of my head have been wiped clean and royalty was placed upon my head. I needed to act accordingly. All the things in my life should have broken me.

I still made it and I'm happy. What should have destroyed me and made my heart turn cold it didn't. I'm still here surviving. I never gave up. All this stuff in my past may have delayed a lot of things in my life but it never denied me access to gifts or the success in my life.

I truly had to step into everything that I deserve. Everything I needed was right on the inside of me. I had to unlearn a lot of things that I was taught that weren't serving my life. I had to learn that being set apart and being different is okay. It's more than okay. I was uniquely made in God's image.

I'm not trading that to be unhappy or be like anyone else. I've learned not to dim my light to make other people feel comfortable. I no longer allow others to push their insecurities on me. I no longer allow others to bash my dreams because they are afraid to chase their own.

I recall my childhood babysitter telling me that when I was a child, she hated me and treated me badly because when she was a teenager she fell in love with my dad, and she became pregnant and was forced to have an abortion. And because I looked so much like my dad, she imagined that her child would have looked like me.

Now, as an adult I was the only one who cared about her and treated her nicely, she felt I needed to know. I asked her what she wanted me to do with that information. I know that sounded mean but the hurt she was carrying had nothing to do with me and the forgiveness she wanted from me she needed to use it to heal herself. I was no longer carrying the burdens of other people. Especially not from my father's past when I wasn't even born when the situation happened.

I say all that to say when God's Grace is shining on you even as a child they try and break your spirit. Through it all

I'm Choosing HAPPY.

I'M Choosing to celebrate life and all my accomplishments.

No matter who doesn't support me. I no longer need validation from anyone else but ME. This journey to happiness was not easy. I know people who still choose to live in misery than to choose to be happy. And that's fine too. We all have choices. I'm proud of myself!!!!

From that 10-year-old girl that used to put rollers in her little miss make-ups doll hair, turn the heat on 90 degrees then place her on the heater to dry. To being cursed out by my mama for touching her heater. Back then all I did was do that doll's hair and write in my diary with the colorful pages that smelled like perfume only for my younger sister to rip the pages out and rub the pages on her arms and neck because she felt like the perfume was going to come off plus it was her way of getting my attention.

To the 13-year-old me that knew she would be a backup dancer for Janet Jackson. I and my friends would practice the Janet Jackson If video all day and night until it was perfect. For no reason. From being in cheer to pom poms and the only Jefferson junior high school mascot that would dance at the assemblies that were doing the splits.

To the 20-year-old me that worked 2 jobs 7 days a week and went to college at the same time because failure was not an option. And now my niece depended on me to be great.

To the 30-year-old me that realized I was doing myself a disservice by not taking care of myself. Knowing that mental health is extremely important. Knowing that just simply going numb to life situations doesn't do anything but hurt you. I recently found out that my grandmother on my mom's side of the family had a mental breakdown that caused her to be hospitalized for a whole year.

In listening to the story, the only question I had is, why didn't she ask for help? My grandmother was amazing. She was a nurse, a hair stylist, and she owned an apartment building. She was so strong but something in her wouldn't allow her to ask for help until she was forced. It made me realize that we are not meant to do everything alone. I recently got a business coach and although I wasn't trusting people. I told her that I was taking a risk because I believed that I was now ready to elevate, and I believed that I had taken my business as far as I could take my business with what I knew and what I researched thus far.

Man. My 30s have been filled with learning lesson after lesson. No Loses just Lessons.

Now in my 40S, I don't want anything more than to continue to just be happy.

No matter what that looks like.

If sitting up at 3 in the morning at my desk listening to old-school R&B.

If it is forcing my family to watch stupid comedy shows that I only enjoy but they know that's what is going to happen if they come to my house.

Happiness looks different for everyone.

Every day won't be an easy one, but it will be worth it if you make choosing happy the choice.

I am now on this happiness journey of becoming a New York Times best-selling Author. So, from this pen to God's ear. I believe it will happen but until then as always, we will continue to glow through whatever it is we are going through.

## Psalm 23:1-6

1 The LORD is my shepherd; I shall not want.

2 He maketh me to lie down in green pastures: he leadeth me beside the still waters.

3 He restoreth my soul: he leadeth me in the paths of righteousness for his name's sake.

4 Yea, though I walk through the valley of the shadow of death, I will fear no evil: for thou art with me; thy rod and thy staff they comfort me.

5 Thou preparest a table before me in the presence of my enemies: thou anointest my head with oil; my cup runneth over.

6 Surely goodness and mercy shall follow me all the days of my life: and I will dwell in the house of the LORD forever.

Made in the USA
Columbia, SC
05 July 2024

19889fa8-8820-4466-9a9a-c96c8fe580d2R01